MESOPOTAMIA

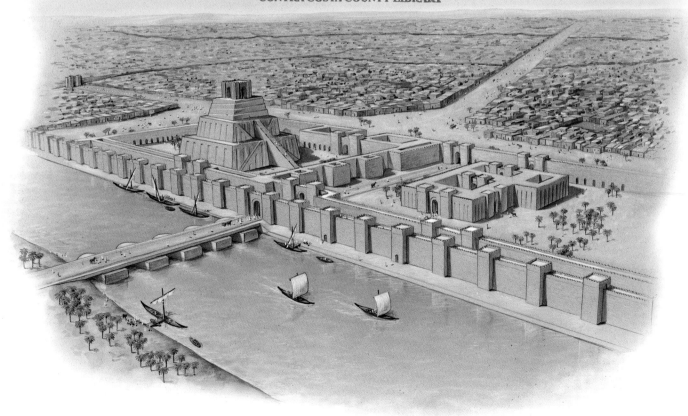

CHELSEA HOUSE
PUBLISHERS
A Haights Cross Communications ⬥ Company ®

First hardcover library edition published
in the United States of America in
2006 by Chelsea House Publishers,
a subsidiary of Haights Cross Communications.
All rights reserved.

A Haights Cross Communications ✈ Company ®

www.chelseahouse.com

Library of Congress Cataloging-in-Publication Data

Bargalló i Chaves, Eva, 1960-
Mesopotamia / Eva Bargalló.
    p. cm. — (Ancient civilizations)
ISBN 0-7910-8604-6 (hardcover)
1. Iraq—Civilization—To 634—Juvenile literature.
I. Title. II. Ancient civilizations (Philadelphia, Pa.).
DS69.5.B33 2005
935—dc2   2004026650

Project and Realization
Parramón Ediciones, S.A.

Texts
Eva Bargalló

Translator
Patrick Clark

Graphic Design and Typesetting
Estudi Toni Inglés (Alba Marco)

Illustrations
Marcel Socías Studio

First edition – February 2004

Printed in Spain
© Parramón Ediciones, S.A. – 2004
Ronda de Sant Pere, 5, 4ª planta
08010 Barcelona (España)
Empresa del Grupo Editorial Norma

www.parramon.com

TABLE OF CONTENTS

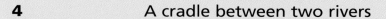
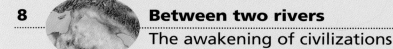

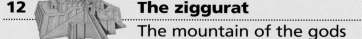

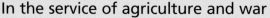
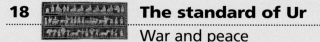

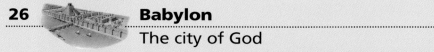

WHERE HISTORY BEGAN

More than four thousand years ago, in a vast region irrigated by the age-old waters of the Tigris and Euphrates rivers, a group of cultures known as Mesopotamian civilization flourished and developed. This civilization stood out not only for its impressive works of art and engineering, but also for its inventiveness and profound capacity for study and observation.

We hope to present young readers with the main features of this passionate culture. The book begins with a brief introduction in the form of a summary. It serves as a spatial and temporal framework for the eleven themes that will be developed in the book. These themes are introduced with a brief presentation and organized around a central image that serves to illustrate, in a clear and concise manner, different aspects of Mesopotamian history and culture. In the same way, the content of each theme is amplified or additional information is offered using additional illustrations.

In order to make reading easier and to complement the information provided, on the last two pages of the book we have included a glossary of terms, a brief chronology, and a list of important people in Mesopotamian history. With regard to the selection of topics and the development of content, attractiveness and appeal took priority over exhaustiveness. Our primary objectives are to awaken in the reader an interest in the history of great civilizations without presenting confusing and excessive historical data and, at the same time, to encourage the reader to dig deeper into the material.

A CRADLE BETWEEN TWO RIVERS

Unlike the Euphrates, the Tigris is a difficult river to tame. Its torrential waters make navigation difficult and limit its use for irrigating fields.

THE GREAT MESOPOTAMIAN CIVILIZATION

Mesopotamia means "between two rivers," specifically the Tigris and the Euphrates, which today flow together in their last stretch to unite with the waters of the Persian Gulf.

Thousands of years ago the land between these rivers formed the cradle of a great civilization. Despite the scarcity of rainfall in this area the soil is very fertile and the characteristics of the Euphrates, from ancient times through today, allow it to be channeled to irrigate the fields and develop the importance of agriculture.

THE SUMERIAN AND AKKADIAN PERIODS

Settlements near the river steadily increased. And the need for irrigation and self-defense eventually led inhabitants to build canals and fortified cities to defend themselves from their enemies.

Sumeria was the first great Mesopotamian civilization. Its people formed a great kingdom consisting of city-states, each headed by a prince. Centuries later the region was conquered by the Akkadians. King Sargon I founded the Akkadian dynasty and created a great state. But Akkadian superiority lasted for only a short time before the Guti invaded the region and hastened the fall of the Akkadians. The Sumerians took advantage of these circumstances to reestablish their city-states. In this way, the Ur dynasty filled a fundamental role and came to dominate a large area of Mesopotamia.

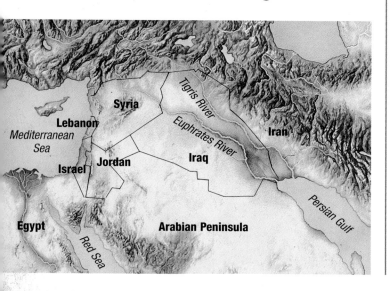

Ancient Mesopotamia extended over the present-day territories of Iraq, Iran, and Syria.

One of the entry gates to the city of Nineveh, seat of one of the most important ancient libraries.

Statue of Gudea, one of the most famous Sumerian leaders of the city-state of Lagash.

THE BABYLONIAN, ASSYRIAN, AND CHALDEAN PERIODS

In later years, the Amorites conquered Sumer and moved the capital of the new kingdom to the city of Babylon. The famous King Hammurabi was responsible for the unification of the Babylonian kingdom, an empire that developed over a period of some four hundred years.

The Babylonians were conquered by the Assyrians, who moved the capital of the kingdom to Nineveh. Their thirst to conquer new territories took them as far as the Mediterranean. The areas they invaded were either annexed or placed under the control of vassal kings.

An intriguing network of Assyrian courtiers and administrators, and attacks by the Medes and Chaldeans, undermined the kingdom and led to its destruction. The Chaldeans took over Mesopotamia and returned capital status and ancient splendor to Babylon, beginning what is known as the neo-Babylonian era. But in the middle of the sixth century B.C., Persia's Cyrus the Great invaded Mesopotamia, putting an end to one of humanity's great civilizations.

A COMPLEX SOCIETY

The Sumerians introduced the main features of Mesopotamian society and culture. Later, the Babylonians and Assyrians followed these traditions, although they adapted them to suit their own needs and ways of thinking. The different people of Mesopotamia were polytheistic and they believed that the gods dominated the different elements on Earth. At the same time, every city had its own local patron god in whose honor a temple was built.

Princes, kings, and priests, who lived in the temple represented the gods and controlled education, commerce, along with the daily and moral lives of the common people.

The economy, religion, social customs, and public life were all regulated by a series of laws that were strictly enforced by the king's officials and the priests. Babylon's King Hammurabi compiled the most complete set of laws of that time.

The Assyrians had invincible military forces and were known and feared for their excessive cruelty on the battlefield.

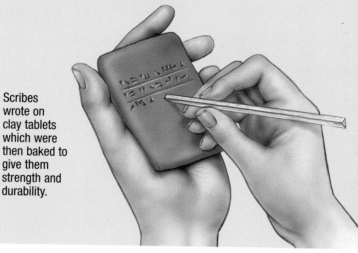
Scribes wrote on clay tablets which were then baked to give them strength and durability.

Despite the severity of some of his decrees, the Assyrians made punishments even tougher and imposed a single code of law and administration throughout the kingdom.

BETWEEN AGRICULTURE AND WAR

During the period of Sumerian domination different social classes based on wealth and social function already existed. Over the years, this differentiation resulted in three categories of people: patricians, the general population, and slaves. The majority of the population dedicated itself to farming and agriculture, the main sources of wealth in Mesopotamia. However, the existence of surplus crops and the need for raw materials led to the development of active trading, which was helped along by the ability to navigate through canals and the river. The exchange of goods generally took place in markets in the cities.

War also played an important role in the daily lives of the people in this region. Frequent attacks and incursions by enemy forces led to the creation of regular armies and fortified cities.

A RICH AND IMAGINATIVE CULTURE

The great cultural contributions of the Sumerians were adopted almost completely by the Babylonians and the Assyrians. It is also important to note that these cultures, particularly during the reign of Hammurabi, were the first to concede the central importance of childhood education.

The development of a complex administration required a system for record keeping and also stimulated the development of writing. But the development of the written word was tied not only to the need to record data and events, but also to the flourishing of rich works of literature with many epic tales.

The ancient inhabitants of Mesopotamia created two inventions that were of critical importance to the development of human civilization: the wheel and the plow. They were also able to develop a complex canal system with dikes, dams, and water tanks in order to irrigate the fields and bring water to the desert.

Thanks to observation and study of the stars, they were able to keep track of

Winged bull with human face that flanked the gates of the Assyrian palace at Khorsabad.

Ceramic pot used to transport oil.

time in months and weeks. They divided the day into twenty-four hours, the hour into sixty minutes, and the minute into sixty seconds. In addition, they gave names to the constellations and assigned a sign of the zodiac to each month of the year.

ART IN THE SERVICE OF POWER AND RELIGION

Various types of Mesopotamian art were intended to glorify the gods and to extol the military victories of the rulers. In the area of architecture, the use of baked bricks allowed for the construction of large buildings such as temples, ziggurats, and palaces.

Cities were made up of narrow streets; houses had two stories, and rooms were organized around a central courtyard. Temples and palaces were the main buildings in the cities. Both were often decorated with beautiful tiles and

mosaics. In addition, palaces were customarily decorated with reliefs and during the Assyrian era they were flanked by immense stone sculptures.

Reliefs usually showed military scenes or hunting scenes. A few scenes that recreated events of everyday life, such as farming or attending festivals, have also been preserved. As a general rule, scenes with animals show a greater affinity for nature than those with human beings, and religious or official artwork is more solemn than works that show scenes from everyday life.

Pottery also played a very important role in Mesopotamian civilization. The use of the potter's wheel and clay firing allowed for the production of large pots, very useful for agriculture and commerce. Small works of art made from metals and inlaid with pearls and precious stones were produced in large quantities, as were small offering statues and cylindrical seals. The seals, used for signing documents, were made with precious stones and wrapped in a strip of moist clay in order to depict a continuous scene in miniature.

THE AWAKENING OF CIVILIZATIONS

The Tigris and the Euphrates, the two rivers that flow into the Persian Gulf, are central players in the rise of civilization in Mesopotamia. Despite the scarcity of rain in most of the region, the waters of these rivers and the fertility of the soil on their banks fostered the development of a rich farming tradition, and the appearance of settlements that, over time, became prosperous and influential cities.

Assyria ■
this nation, despite having a culture very similar to that of Babylonia, stood out for its extreme cruelty

metallurgy ■
the Mesopotamians worked with several metals including bronze, copper, and gold; they made tools, including knives or nails, with these materials

agriculture ■
the development of land cultivation favored the invention and use of tools such as the plow pulled by oxen

Mediterranean Sea

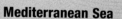

ADOBE, A BASIC MATERIAL

It is a clump of mud sometimes mixed with straw and dried in the open air. The soil of Mesopotamia is rich in adobe, and its inhabitants baked it in order to obtain the terracotta used to make pieces of pottery, sculpture, and tablets for writing. It was also the main material used for the construction of houses and other buildings. Adobe that was not mixed with straw was used to make bricks that were baked to make them stronger and more resistant.

Red Sea

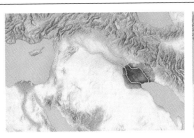
Maximum extent of Sumer.

Maximum extent of Assyria.

Maximum extent of the Babylonian empire.

Nineveh ■
capital of the Assyrian empire: it used a system of canals and aqueducts to bring water to its inhabitants

■ **construction**
the Mesopotamians were the first to bake bricks which they used to build their houses and other buildings

Euphrates River

Tigris River

Sippar

Susa

Nippur

Uruk   Lagash

Babylon ■
the capital of the Babylonian empire; home to one of the Seven Wonders of the Ancient World: the Hanging Gardens

Ur ■
one of the most important city-states of the Sumerian empire; very valuable archaeological remains from this city have been preserved

Persian Gulf

Babylonian empire ■
the Babylonians developed a political structure headed by a king who exercised legislative, judicial, and executive power as an absolute monarch

■ **Sumeria**
the first of the great Mesopotamian civilizations made up of several city-states

THE SYMBOL OF POWER AND PROGRESS

In general, Mesopotamian cities were built beside or near the river, and canals were built to bring water to the crops. The main buildings, such as royal palaces or temples, were built inside fortified enclosures. Houses of citizens were also inside. Most citizens worked in agriculture, although some were involved in trade or craftsmanship.

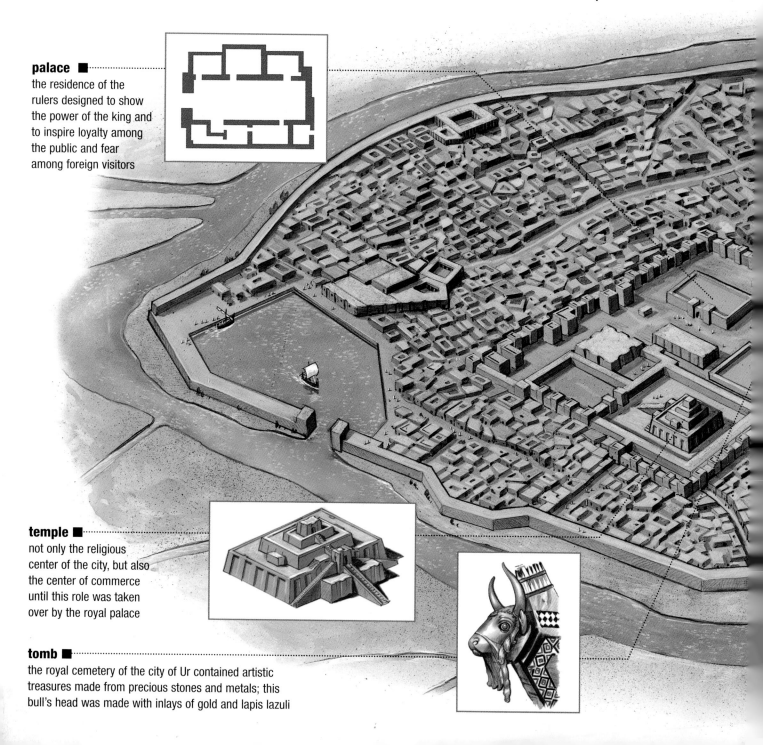

palace ■
the residence of the rulers designed to show the power of the king and to inspire loyalty among the public and fear among foreign visitors

temple ■
not only the religious center of the city, but also the center of commerce until this role was taken over by the royal palace

tomb ■
the royal cemetery of the city of Ur contained artistic treasures made from precious stones and metals; this bull's head was made with inlays of gold and lapis lazuli

TOGETHER UNTIL DEATH

One of the most spectacular discoveries made during the excavations in the ancient Sumerian city of Ur was the royal cemetery. Findings made in this place showed that the death of a king and his wife was followed by the voluntary death of members of the court.

■ **house**
rooms were usually grouped around a central uncovered courtyard; excess water was removed using pipes

■ **trade**
mercantile activity developed mainly around the temple whose warehouses were the wealthiest of the city; heavier merchandise was transported with the help of a wagon

■ **canal**
a complex system of canals was used to irrigate the fields, transport goods, and control the flow of the river

■ **port**
boats loaded with goods such as barley, precious stones, wood, copper, and ivory arrived in the ports to sell and trade in city markets

■ **wall**
cities were fortified to defend them against attacks by enemies; bricks made from baked adobe were the main construction material used

THE MOUNTAIN OF THE GODS

Between the fourth millennium and the year 600 B.C. large towers in honor of the local gods were built next to temples in the city-states of Mesopotamia. It is believed that these monumental watchtowers, called ziggurats, were mainly intended to shorten the distance between the priests or sovereigns and the gods, or to serve as a platform so that the deities could come down from their home in the sky to visit humanity. It is also believed that they were used as an observatory to study the stars.

materials ■
ziggurats were built from a core of sun-dried bricks that were then covered with baked bricks

decoration ■
on some occasions the walls of these great towers were covered with brightly glazed bricks

pyramid structure ■
the ziggurat grew out of different stories placed over a large platform; the walls of these stories were slightly inclined toward the interior

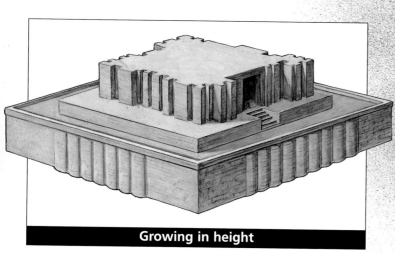

Growing in height

The first Mesopotamian temples were built on platforms of adobe bricks. Later these platforms became taller until the temples stood out over the houses. The faithful entered using stairways.

THE TOWER OF BABEL

Babel is the biblical name for Babylon. According to the Holy Scriptures, the Tower of Babel was intended to reach heaven. In order to prevent this, God mixed up the languages of the workers on the colossal tower, and scattered them throughout the territory. This beautiful story was inspired by the ziggurat of Etemenanki in Babylon.

■ **gigunu**

the highest room or temple of a ziggurat was a room devoted to the relaxation of the deity after his descent to Earth

■ **floors**

some ziggurats, such as that of Babylon, rose to six or seven stories; generally, the height of a ziggurat was lower, like that of Ur, which originally had three stories

stairs ■

different stairways led to the small sanctuary at the top of the ziggurat

HEAVEN, HELL, AND THE EARTH

The people of Mesopotamia believed that the world was controlled by gods, some beneficent and some with ill intentions. These deities controlled the elements of Earth such as water, fire, or air. Cities also had their own patron divinities that they worshipped in big temples. The warehouses of these sacred places were usually the richest in the city; their wealth came from donations by citizens or from harvesting their own crops.

THE CREATION OF MANKIND

According to a Mesopotamian legend, the gods, tired of working, decided to create creatures out of mud who would take their place in doing the most difficult jobs: these creatures were human beings. From that moment, human beings became servants of the gods, laboring on behalf of the gods in the fields and sharing food and drink with them through offerings.

Sin ■
god of passing time, god of the lunar cycle

Anu ■
god of the sky, father of the gods

Zababa ■
god of war and patron of the Akkadian city of Kush

Nergal ■
god of hell, lord of the underworld

Priests were the representatives of the gods on Earth and they lived in the temple. From this place, the economic center of the city, they controlled daily life and the morality of the people.

Priests

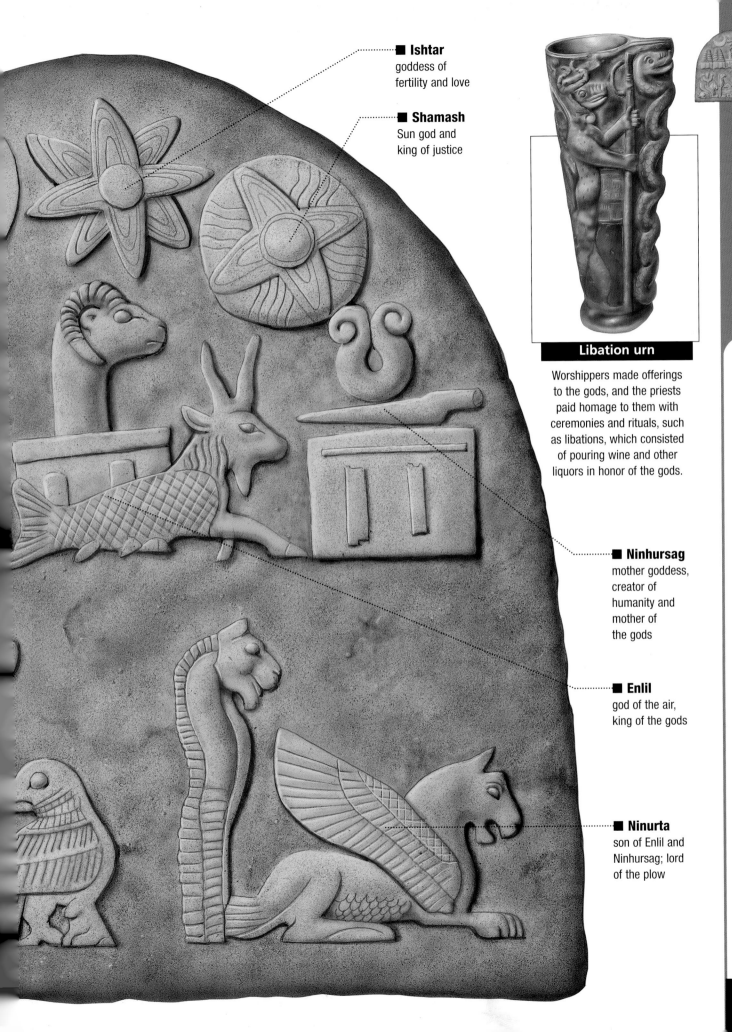

■ **Ishtar**
goddess of
fertility and love

■ **Shamash**
Sun god and
king of justice

Libation urn

Worshippers made offerings
to the gods, and the priests
paid homage to them with
ceremonies and rituals, such
as libations, which consisted
of pouring wine and other
liquors in honor of the gods.

■ **Ninhursag**
mother goddess,
creator of
humanity and
mother of
the gods

■ **Enlil**
god of the air,
king of the gods

■ **Ninurta**
son of Enlil and
Ninhursag; lord
of the plow

IN THE SERVICE OF AGRICULTURE AND WAR

The inhabitants of Mesopotamia were imaginative people, able to create great works of engineering and architecture and to invent such things as the wheel or the plow which were so important in the progress of humanity. They also played a key role in the spread and use of bronze and other materials such as brick, and they invented such useful machines as the potter's wheel, which brought about a decisive change in the quality and production of pottery.

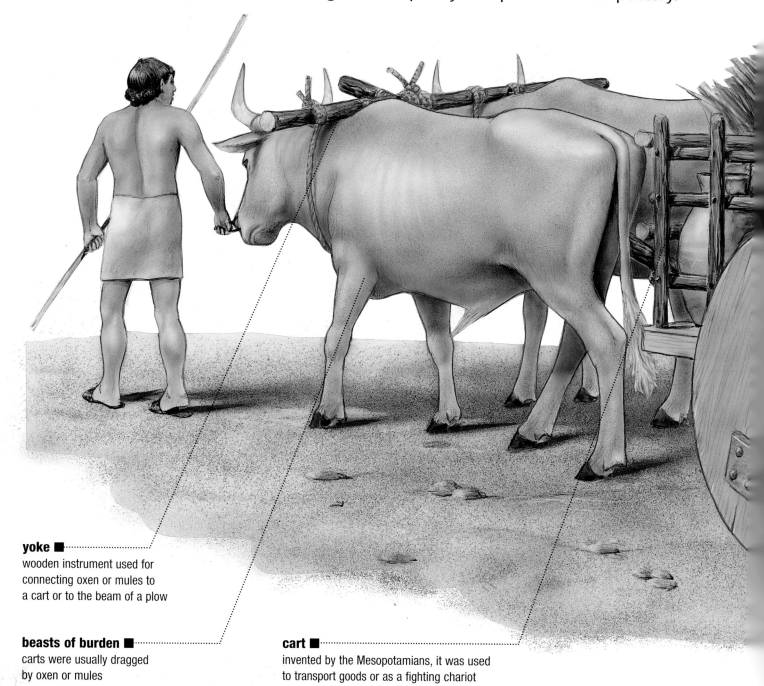

yoke ■
wooden instrument used for connecting oxen or mules to a cart or to the beam of a plow

beasts of burden ■
carts were usually dragged by oxen or mules

cart ■
invented by the Mesopotamians, it was used to transport goods or as a fighting chariot

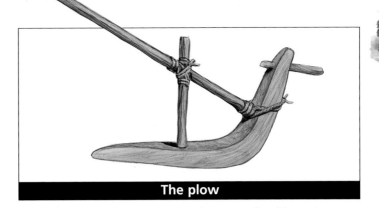

WATER TAMERS

The Mesopotamians converted river marshes into plains suitable for cultivation. Similarly, they opened canals to irrigate the fields and transport goods, and they constructed an extensive network of drains in order to remove excess water from the cities.

The plow

Before its creation, fields were usually very small and harvests were uncertain. The use of the plow revolutionized agriculture because it allowed for the ventilation of the soil and the burial of the remains of old crops, making harvests more abundant.

■ **load**
carts transported goods such as grains, cloth, metals, or bricks

■ **construction material**
carts were made with pieces of wood fastened with copper nails or pegs also made of wood

■ **nails**
copper nails were used in Mesopotamia to fasten the wood on carts and other devices

■ **wheel**
invented around the year 3500 B.C., it allowed for the construction of machines such as the potter's wheel or means of transportation such as the cart

WAR AND PEACE

This masterpiece of Mesopotamian art, found in the royal cemetery of Ur, consists of four flat pieces decorated with a mosaic of lapis lazuli, inlaid with mollusk shells and pearls. The two main surfaces are divided into three parts, and represent scenes relating to war and peace. The importance of the Standard of Ur lies not only in the quality of its execution and its iconic nature, but also in its narrative value.

soldiers ■
dressed in cloth or wool tunics; sometimes they wore copper helmets and used different types of arms, such as lances, axes, or daggers

cart ■
drivers guided their carts with reins that were secured to the donkey's back and nose

sovereign ■
kings protected the city in the name of the local divinity

BOTTOM TO TOP
The story in these two panels begins at the left in the bottom row and finishes at the top.

clothing ■
attendees at the celebration wear the typical Sumerian skirt and bare their chests

harp ■
musical instruments were often made with valuable materials and were decorated with scenes showing people and animals

singer ■
music and song played an important role in celebrations

■ **materials**
the standard of Ur was achieved mainly with lapis lazuli and pearl inlays

■ **sheep**
in great demand because their wool was used to make fabric

■ **oxen**
used to pull carts or plows

WAR

This panel tells the story of a battle with war chariots. In the bottom row the king, mounted on his chariot, appears in four successive moments from the time the animals begin to walk until they are galloping. In the middle row soldiers lead away prisoners. In the top row, soldiers bring defeated troops before the king who is placed in the middle of the scene; at left, the royal squire controls the cart with reins.

PEACE

In the lower and middle rows of the panel above, servants transport delicacies and animals for sacrifice to celebrate victory over the enemies. The top row depicts a banquet: the king drinks in the company of other important people, accompanied by the music of a lyre and songs.

THE IMMORTALITY OF WORDS

Around the third millennium B.C., the inhabitants of Mesopotamia developed a form of writing in order to record aspects of their economy and social life in the community. This writing was based on pictograms, which, as the years passed, evolved until they became cuneiform signs. Cuneiform, which gets its name because its signs have the form of a cradle (*cuna* in Latin), was usually inscribed on clay tablets; however, inscriptions have also been found on metal and stone objects.

■ **pictograms**
drawings that represent
a word or phrase

calamus ■
beveled reed that was used to trace
inscriptions on clay tables and gave
the typical cradle shape to the signs

a	gin/gub	anse	mu_er	gu	_ag	gi
water	walk	donkey	bird	ox	head	reed

■ **cuneiform signs**
over time, pictograms evolved into
abstract signs, allowing more complex
ideas and concepts to be represented

■ **number of signs**
cuneiform writing had more than 900
characters and throughout its development
never had less than 400 symbols

scribes

In Mesopotamia scribes enjoyed great prestige. Because they were specialists in writing, they were entrusted with recording registries and administrative and commercial documents.

How to read a pictograph

Pictographs were written inside rectangles placed in rows that were read from right to left and from top to bottom.

■ **record keeping**

the development of writing in Mesopotamia was due in large measure to the need to keep track of the quantity of grain in each harvest; similarly, information related to the activities of the temple, trade, and transactions was also noted

ONE SYSTEM AND MANY LANGUAGES

The cuneiform system was invented by the Sumerians so that they could write in their own language. But this type of writing was also adopted for use with other languages in other cultures, such as the Akkadians, the Babylonians, the Assyrians, the Hittites, the Luwites, and the Hurrites.

se	ku	ud	dug	su	gisimmar	ku
barley	eat	day	pot	hand	palm tree	fish

■ **tablets**

made out of moist clay; upon finishing the writing, they were left to dry in the sun or baked to harden them

■ **literature**

beautiful stories and legends, such as that of the hero Gilgamesh, were also written in cuneiform symbols

A FANTASTIC COLLECTION OF LAWS

King Hammurabi of Babylon ordered that the 282 rules of his famous code be recorded on a block of black stone a few yards high in order to form a list of all the civil and criminal laws existing at the time. To stress the divine origin of the laws, the image of the king receiving the code from the hands of the god Shamash was shown on the top part of the stone. The main purpose for compiling these laws was to regulate all aspects of Babylonian society, from property and family to trade and public works.

Hammurabi of Babylon

In addition to compiling the laws that governed daily life in his kingdom, Hammurabi turned Babylon into a great empire and an important center of trade. He personally supervised the collection of taxes and the building of temples, and controlled navigation, irrigation, and agriculture, the most important areas of the economy.

A HIERARCHICAL SOCIETY

The decrees of Hammurabi's Code start out with the idea of three very different social classes: the *awilum*, or patricians; the *muskenum*, or the general public; and the *wardum*, or slaves.

AN EYE FOR AN EYE

Hammurabi's Code was very severe. Here are a few examples:

• If a man has put out the eye of a free person, his eye will also be taken out.

• If a man has put out the eye of the slave of a free man, he shall pay half the price of the slave.

• If a man is found committing acts of robbery, he shall be put to death.

king ■
Hammurabi was a great ruler; the time under his rule has been defined as "The Golden Age of Babylon"

laws ■
the Code of Hammurabi consists of 282 laws and decrees that summarize all the civil and criminal laws of the time

code ■
a group of laws that adhere to a methodological and systematic procedure

structure ■
the text of the code, written in cuneiform, is distributed on the surface of the stone in 44 horizontal columns: 16 on the front and 28 on the back

■ **diorite**
dark-colored rock used as a surface to record the precepts decreed by Hammurabi

■ **god**
Shamash, the Mesopotamian god of the sun and of justice, passes down the laws to Hammurabi

■ **stele**
a monument built in the ground in the shape of a tombstone or pedestal; Hammurabi ordered his code to be recorded on steles that were distributed throughout the kingdom

THE LEARNED KING

Assurbanipal was the last great ruler of Assyria. Famous for great military exploits that allowed him to extend his kingdom up to the south of Egypt and to the west of Anatolia, he was also a patron of the arts and literature. During his reign, Assyrian culture reached its high point and the famous library of Nineveh, founded by Sargon II, was expanded to include some one hundred thousand volumes.

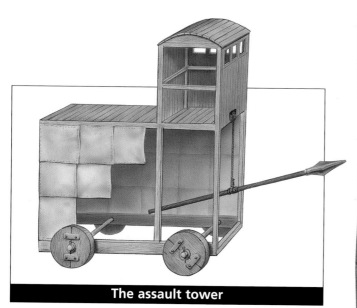

The assault tower

This device, conceived by the Assyrians, made of wood and covered with animal skins to hide the archers who traveled inside it, facilitated the entry of soldiers into fortified areas.

A GREAT COLLECTION

Assurbanipal's library in Nineveh housed the first cataloged collection of manuscripts. In his eagerness to create a huge library, this king sent scribes to different parts of the kingdom to copy ancient Sumerian texts on clay tablets.

■ **literature**
the library in Nineveh housed great treasures of Mesopotamian literature, such as the familiar epic of Gilgamesh

■ **Nineveh**
capital of the Assyrian empire on the shores of the Tigris River; a religious, artistic, and cultural center; after being pillaged by the Babylonians and the Medes it never recovered its ancient splendor

■ **Assurbanipal**
also known as Sardanapalus, he was the king of Assyria between 669 and 627 B.C.

Hunting a lion

Many of the reliefs that decorate the palace of Assurbanipal in Nineveh depict scenes from the daily life of the king. He may appear on horseback, raised up in a cart, or on foot hunting a lion.

■ **war**
Assyrian kings were the leaders of the army who directed military campaigns; the conquered lands were ruled by governors

■ **relief**
the Assyrians covered the walls of their palaces with magnificent relief sculptures that depicted scenes of war and hunting

THE CITY OF GOD

Babylon, known primarily for its huge ziggurat and its mythical hanging gardens, was one of the most important cities of ancient times, as well as the religious and administrative capital of the great Babylonian kingdom. Defended by imposing walls and fortified gates, it was the site of rich palaces, temples, and paved procession roads. It was destroyed by King Sennacherib of Assyria in 689 B.C. and later rebuilt by his successor, Esarhaddon.

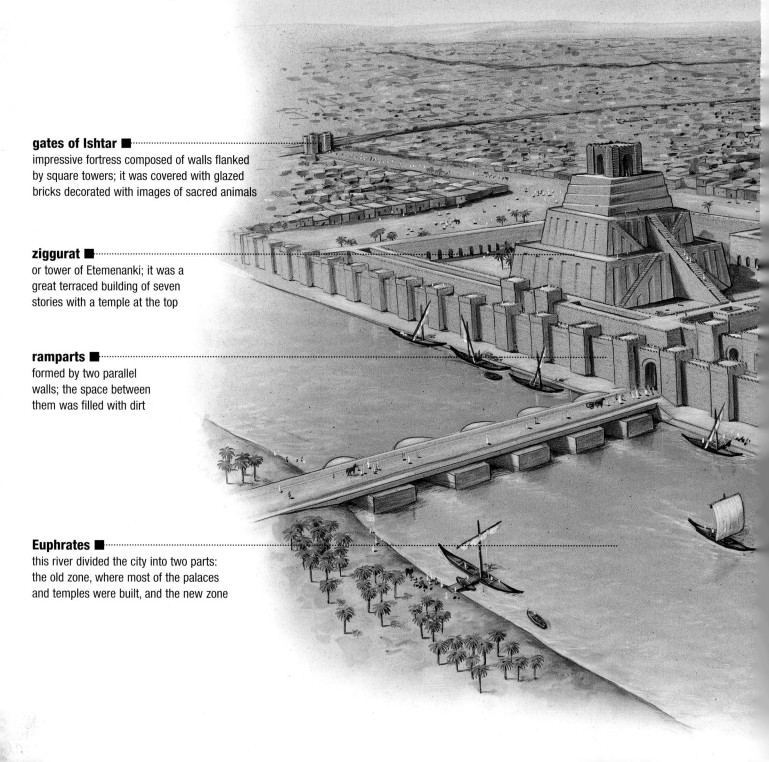

gates of Ishtar ■
impressive fortress composed of walls flanked by square towers; it was covered with glazed bricks decorated with images of sacred animals

ziggurat ■
or tower of Etemenanki; it was a great terraced building of seven stories with a temple at the top

ramparts ■
formed by two parallel walls; the space between them was filled with dirt

Euphrates ■
this river divided the city into two parts: the old zone, where most of the palaces and temples were built, and the new zone

THE HANGING GARDENS OF BABYLON

Some say that Nebuchadnezzar II wanted to give his wife a gift that would express his great love for her. So, he had a series of gardened terraces built over a large area to form a kind of artificial mountain. These gardens were located beside the king's palace, next to the river. On top of the highest terrace was a water tank used to irrigate this magnificent garden.

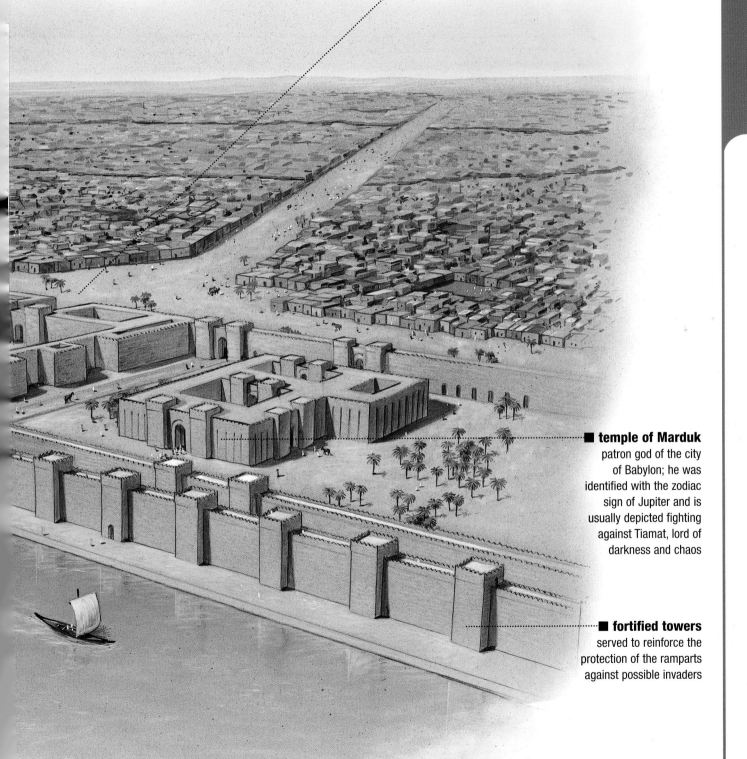

■ **processional avenue**
this great thoroughfare crossed the city from the Ishtar gate to the great ziggurat; it was the road that priests and rulers followed during religious ceremonies

■ **temple of Marduk**
patron god of the city of Babylon; he was identified with the zodiac sign of Jupiter and is usually depicted fighting against Tiamat, lord of darkness and chaos

■ **fortified towers**
served to reinforce the protection of the ramparts against possible invaders

HEROES AND GODS

This beautiful Sumerian poem, best known for an Assyrian version and written with cuneiform characters, is considered a masterpiece of Mesopotamian literature. Its importance rests, above all, in being one of the first examples of literature in history, and in constituting a profound reflection about humanity. It is also important for its descriptions of the main characteristics of the civilization that developed in lower Mesopotamia.

■ gods
many of the characters that appear in this poem are gods, among them Ishtar, goddess of fertility and love; Enlil, responsible for floods; and Ea, patron of humanity and god of the arts

story line ■
this poem narrates the adventures of Gilgamesh, king of Uruk, and his friend Enkidu, in their search for glory and immortality; Enkidu ends up dying, and Gilgamesh finally resigns himself to his human fate

the worldwide flood ■
the epic of Gilgamesh also includes the Mesopotamian legend of the worldwide flood; in this version, the hero, Utnapishtim, corresponds to Noah in the biblical version; by order of the god Ea, Utnapishtim builds a boat to save himself and his family from the flood

THE NUMBER SIX

The epic of Gilgamesh is structured around the sexagesimal number system, a system based on the number six and its multiples and factors. Similarly, the text is divided into twelve tablets, which in turn are each divided into six columns; each tablet has an average length of 300 verses.

■ **epic poem**
a narrative written in verse that describes legendary or royal events; it frequently includes supernatural beings, heroes, and battle descriptions

heroes ■
the protagonists of legends and epic poems admired for their bravery and their personal qualities; in this poem the three main heroes are Gilgamesh, Enkidu, and Utnapishtim

Gilgamesh ■ ·······························
legendary king of the Sumerian city of Uruk; the main protagonist of this epic: a hero who seeks immortality because he does not resign himself to the human condition

Sumerian language ■
this poem was originally written in the Sumerian language, a language that, to this day, has not been classified within any of the known large linguistic families

GLOSSARY

Absolute monarchy	Political system in which the king is all-powerful, with no legal limitations on his power.
Adobe	Block of earth, mainly clay, dried in the sun.
City-state	City whose independent government makes it similar to a small state.
Cuneiform writing	Characters used by the Mesopotamian people for writing; they resemble small triangles and are written on clay tablets.
Epic	Long narrative poem that relates praiseworthy deeds and heroic characters.
Iconography	Study of the images in art.
Pictogram	Drawing that represents an object or an idea.
Polytheism	Belief in the existence of many gods.
Relief	Sculpture that sticks out on a flat surface.
Terracotta	Pottery made of baked earth.
Ziggurat	Sanctuary in the form of a tower common to Mesopotamian architecture.

CHRONOLOGY

3500 B.C.	The Sumerian people, coming from Central Asia, found the first Mesopotamian cities.
3200 B.C.	Pictographic writing.
2400 B.C.	Cuneiform writing.
2300 B.C.	The Akkadians, a Semitic people from central Mesopotamia, conquer the area. Sargon I unites the Sumerian cities into a kingdom.
2200 B.C.	Expansion and decline of the Akkadian empire.
2100 B.C.	Ur, capital of the new Sumerian kingdom.
2000 B.C.	The Elamites destroy the city of Ur.
1800 B.C.	Hammurabi of Babylon unifies Mesopotamia.
1225 B.C.	The Assyrians conquer the Babylonian empire.
1000 B.C.	The Assyrians reach as far as the Mediterranean.
730–650 B.C.	Maximum extent of the Assyrian empire.
600 B.C.	Assyria is destroyed by the Chaldeans. Nebuchadnezzar II reconstructs Babylon.
500 B.C.	Mesopotamia is conquered by the Persians.

TO KNOW MORE

IMPORTANT PEOPLE

Sargon I

This powerful king, known as Sargon the Great, was the founder of the kingdom and the dynasty of Akkad. His great deeds on the field of battle culminated with the unification of Sumer and Akkad, and control of the great trade routes.

Naram-Sin

This Akkadian king, grandson of Sargon I, gave himself the title "King of Four Nations," and proclaimed himself a god. The story of his military victories is told in a famous stele that bears his name.

Gudea

The most famous ruler of the Sumerian city of Lagash. During his rule, he tried to avoid armed conflicts with neighboring cities. Many surviving sculptures that serve as a rich source of information about Sumerian culture show him in prayer and bear inscriptions.

Gudea

Hammurabi

In addition to being an extraordinary lawmaker, this king, the most prestigious of the Babylonian empire, stood out for his military prowess and as a very capable administrator.

Senaquerib

Assyrian monarch, outstanding for his warlike character and military campaigns in Egypt. He rebuilt the city of Nineveh and provided it with a fortress with beautiful palaces and temples. According to Muslim tradition, the tomb of the prophet Jonah is inside one of the palaces.

Hammurabi

Assurbanipal

The last of the great Assyrian rulers extended his empire as far as the south of Egypt and the western part of Anatolia. He was a very cultured man; during his time as king he assembled a large library and decorated his royal residences with large relief sculptures depicting scenes of war, hunting, and daily life.

Nabucodonosor II

He was the most important monarch of the neo-Babylonian dynasty. Under his leadership the empire became the main military power in the Near East. However his fame is, above all, due to one particular event: the capture of Jerusalem and the subsequent transport of thousands of Jewish prisoners to Babylon.

Assurbanipal

INDEX